The

SHORTEST DAY
CELEBRATING THE WINTER SOLSTICE

Wendy Pfeffer

illustrated by

Jesse Reisch

PUFFIN BOOKS
An Imprint of Penguin Group (USA)

ACKNOWLEDGMENTS

*With sincere thanks to Dr. James C. White, Professor of Physics at Rhodes College,
and a fellow of both the International Astronomical Union and Great Britain's Royal Astronomical Society,
for so generously sharing his expertise and to Dr. Derek Peterson, Professor of History
at the College of New Jersey, for his expert comments.*

*With thanks also to Stephanie Owens Lurie, my editor and friend;
Andrea Merrick and Amy Miele, patient and persistent research librarians;
and my readers Sally Bridwell, Tim, Jaime, and Diane Kianka.*

PUFFIN BOOKS
Published by the Penguin Group
Penguin Group (USA) LLC
375 Hudson Street
New York, New York 10014

USA ★ Canada ★ UK ★ Ireland ★ Australia
New Zealand ★ India ★ South Africa ★ China

penguin.com
A Penguin Random House Company

First published in the United States of America by Dutton Children's Books,
a division of Penguin Young Readers Group, 2003
Published by Puffin Books, an imprint of Penguin Young Readers Group, 2014

Text copyright © 2003 by Wendy Pfeffer
Illustrations copyright © 2003 by Jesse Reisch

THE LIBRARY OF CONGRESS HAS CATALOGED THE DUTTON CHILDREN'S BOOKS EDITION AS FOLLOWS:
Pfeffer, Wendy, date.
The shortest day : celebrating the winter solstice / by Wendy Pfeffer;
Illustrated by Jesse Reisch.—1st ed.
p. cm.
Summary: Describes how and why daylight grows shorter as winter approaches, the effect of shorter days on
animals and people, and how the winter solstice has been celebrated throughout history. Includes activities.
ISBN 978-0-525-46968-1 (hardcover)
1. Winter solstice—Juvenile literature. 2. Winter festivals—Juvenile literature.
[1. Winter solstice. 2. Winter festivals. 3. Festivals.] I. Reisch, Jesse, ill. II. Title.
GT4995.W55P44 2003
394.261—dc21
2003040811

Puffin Books ISBN 978-0-14-751284-0

9 10 8
Manufactured in China

For Steve, Diane, Mark, Jennifer,
Sharon, Johnny, Kirsten, Paul, Erik, and Jill,
several of whom are fine writers

—W.P.

To BSR, with great love and gratitude

—J.R.

In late autumn

in the northern part of the world,

squirrels hide nuts,

foxes grow thick fur coats,

and flocks of birds fly to warmer places.

The sun rises later each morning
and sets earlier each evening.
Each day it appears lower in the southern sky.

As the sun gets lower and lower,
the north gets less and less daylight.
The air grows colder.

Chickadees fluff their feathers to keep warm.
Woodchucks hibernate in their burrows,
and white-tailed deer nuzzle through the snow
to find the last blades of grass.

On short winter days,
children bundle in warm clothes
and walk through a frosty white world,
dragging long shadows behind them.

On long winter nights,
families eat dinner while it's dark outside.
Children wonder when the days will get long again
so they can play outside after dinner,
like they did in summer.

In the north, on or around December 21,
the sun reaches its lowest point on the horizon,
making that day the shortest day of the year.
Like all days, December 21
has twenty-four hours.
But it's called the shortest day
because it has the fewest hours of daylight.

The shortest day, called the winter solstice,
is the beginning of winter.
And in some places winter means
cold, nose-nipping weather.

The earth tilts as it moves around the sun.
When the northern part of the earth
tilts away from the sun,
the north gets less heat and light
than the southern part.

Long ago, people didn't understand
how the earth tilts and moves around the sun.
They didn't understand
why each day had less sunshine than the day before.
Some believed that evil spirits made the sun go away.

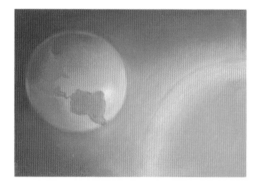

People feared
that the sun wouldn't shine on them anymore,
making their world cold and dreary dark.
They needed the sun's warmth and light.
So did their plants, which they needed for food.
They held ceremonies that lasted for weeks
to persuade their gods to bring the sun back.

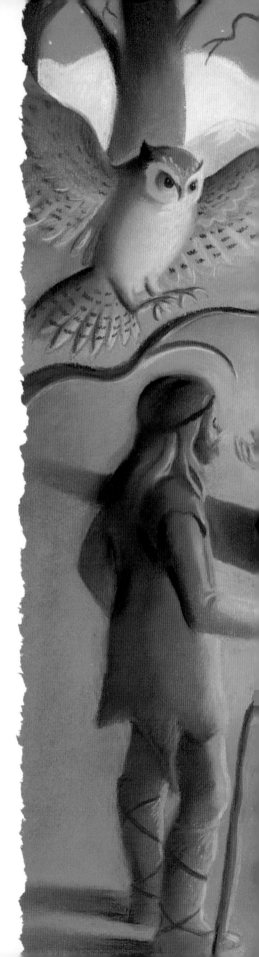

Over the years people noticed
that after short days,
the days got gradually longer.
Joyous people bathed
in the sun's warmth and light.

They celebrated their harvests.

About 5,000 years ago,
people who studied the sky
noticed that day after day
the sun set in different places
on the western horizon.
They discovered that
when the sun set farthest south,
that was the shortest day.

These early astronomers
planned to mark the shortest day.
Then each year people would know
when the days would start getting
longer again.

On the day when the sun reached
its southernmost point on the horizon,
the astronomers carried out their plan.
Workers stacked stones to frame the setting sun.
They made a special opening,
like a keyhole or the eye of a needle.
When the setting sun's rays
beamed through that opening,
people knew the shortest day was over.

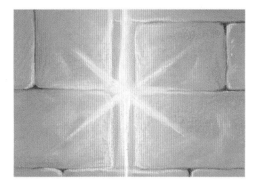

Days gradually got longer
for the next six months.
When the sun appeared farthest to the north,
its rays shone through another "keyhole."
People knew it was the longest day of the year,
the first day of summer.

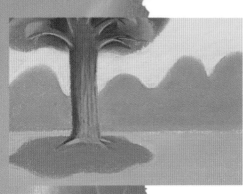

In China, over 3,000 years ago,
astronomers measured shadows
to determine the shortest day.
The longest shadows appeared
on the shortest day
because the sun was at
its lowest point in the sky.

They knew that as the sun appeared
higher in the sky,
the shadows would get shorter,
and the days would get longer.

Over 2,000 years ago,
Romans celebrated the shortest day
with festivals and merrymaking.
They gave evergreen branches to friends
as a sign of good luck.
Evergreen wreaths decorated their doors.
Since these plants stayed green
when others turned brown,
they reminded the Romans
of the coming spring.

Mistletoe and holly hung in their homes,
because plants that survived the harsh winter
were symbols of life.
Many people believed these plants
would bring strength to their families.

About 1,000 years ago,
Europeans celebrated the winter solstice.
Druid priests of England and Ireland
decorated oak trees
with golden apples and candles
to represent harvest and light.

In Sweden, a festival of light
celebrated the return of longer days.
On St. Lucia's Day,
girls wore crowns
of evergreens and candles
to rekindle the sun's fire
as they delivered warm buns
to family and friends.
Boys went from door to door,
singing to the neighbors
for a few coins.

Around the same time in history,
the Incas of Peru marked the shortest day
with a festival in honor of the sun.
At dawn, when the sun first appeared,
shouts of happiness rang out.
Then the Incas used a shiny surface
to reflect the sun's rays
onto fluffy, dry cotton.
The sun heated the cotton
and made it burst into flame.

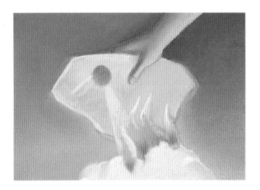

They carried the fire to their temples
and kept it burning on the altars all year,
because it came from one of their gods,
the sun.

Today people still celebrate
at the beginning of winter
by decorating their houses,
lighting the darkness,
gathering together,
and exchanging gifts.

They no longer worry
that the sun will disappear forever.
People know that days get colder
when their part of the earth
tilts away from the sun.
They know that days get shorter
when the sun appears lower in the sky.

People celebrate the shortest day
because longer days follow.
Flocks of birds will return,
seedling oak trees will sprout,
and children can play outside after dinner.

For more than 5,000 years,
people have welcomed the winter solstice
because it's a new beginning.

Solstice Facts

The earth is always spinning, like a top. It takes 24 hours for the earth to turn one time. When the earth turns toward the sun, it's day. When it turns away from the sun, it's night.

It takes 12 months for the earth to go around the sun. The tilt of the earth on its axis as it rotates determines how the sun's rays hit the earth and what season it is.

Over 750 years ago, the word *solstice* was first used for the time when the *sun* seemed to *stop* moving. *Solstice* comes from Latin, the language of the ancient Romans. In Latin, *sol* means "sun," and *sistere* means "to stop."

In the northern part of the world, the winter solstice usually occurs on December 21, but the earth doesn't move at a steady speed around the sun, so sometimes the winter solstice occurs on December 20, 22, or 23.

Equinox comes from two Latin words. *Aequi* means "equal," and *nox* means "night." On the spring equinox and autumn equinox, day and night have equal hours.

WINTER
The northern part of the earth tilts away from the sun, and the sun is lowest in the sky. It's the winter solstice, with the shortest day and longest night. Every place within 400 miles of the North Pole has 24 hours of darkness.

SPRING
Three months later, the north and south are the same distance from the sun, and the sun shines on the middle of the earth. It's the spring equinox. Days and nights are of equal length.

AUTUMN

Another three months later, the north and south are the same distance from the sun, and the sun shines on the middle of the earth. It's the autumn equinox. Days and nights are of equal length.

SUMMER

Three months after that, the northern part of the earth tilts toward the sun, and the sun is highest in the sky. It's the summer solstice, with the longest day and shortest night. Every place within 400 miles of the North Pole has 24 hours of daylight.

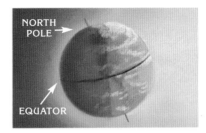

WINTER SOLSTICE

The sun is low in the sky and shining from its southernmost position.

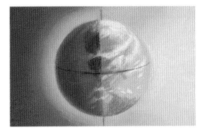

SPRING EQUINOX

SUMMER SOLSTICE

The sun is high in the sky and shining from its northernmost position.

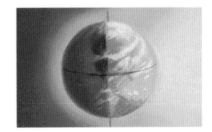

AUTUMN EQUINOX

Above are the seasons in the Northern Hemisphere.

MAKE A WINTER SUNRISE/SUNSET CHART

What you need:

- a pencil and a colored marker
- four copies of the chart below
- a daily newspaper
- tape

What to do:

1. List the times on your copies of the chart below.
2. Write in the dates you are going to chart.
3. Find the sunrise and sunset times in each day's newspaper
4. Record the sunrise time.
5. Record the sunset time.
6. Color in the hours between sunrise and sunset.
7. Tape four weekly charts together, in order.

If you faithfully chart the sunrise and sunset times for a month, your chart will show an interesting shape!

TIME OF DAY

5:30 P.M.							
5:20 P.M.							
5:10 P.M.							
5:00 P.M.							
4:50 P.M.							
4:40 P.M.							
4:30 P.M.							
4:20 P.M.							
4:10 P.M.							
4:00 P.M.							
3:00 P.M.							
2:00 P.M.							
1:00 P.M.							
12:00 P.M.							
11:00 A.M.							
10:00 A.M.							
9:00 A.M.							
8:00 A.M.							
7:30 A.M.							
7:20 A.M.							
7:10 A.M.							
7:00 A.M.							
6:50 A.M.							
6:40 A.M.							
6:30 A.M.							
6:20 A.M.							
6:10 A.M.							
6:00 A.M.							
	DATE	DATE	DATE	DATE	DATE	DATE	DATE

MEASURE SHADOWS ON THE SHORTEST DAY

What you need:

- a tape measure
- paper and pencil

Around December 21 (you'll need a sunny day):

1. At noon, stand outside in a sunny spot.
2. Ask a friend to measure your shadow on the ground, using the tape measure.
3. Record the place, date, time; the length of your shadow; and whether the sun was high or low in the sky.
4. Measure other shadows, such as a tree or a mailbox.
5. Record as in step 3.

Around March 21, June 21, and
September 21, repeat steps 1 to 5.
Note the differences.

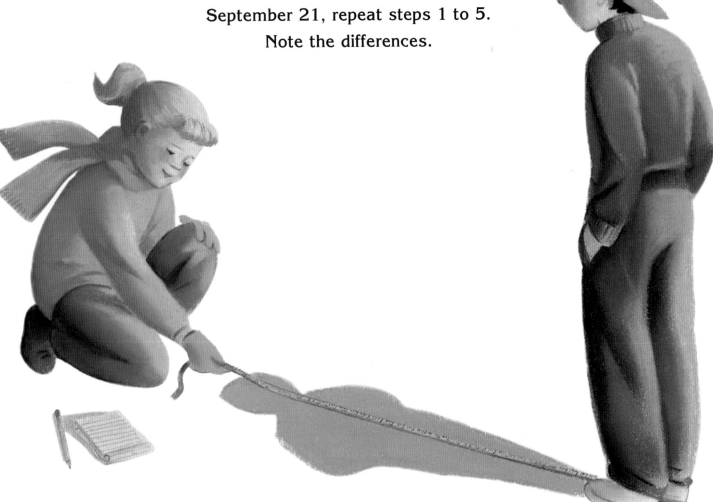

FIND THE SUN'S
NORTHERNMOST AND SOUTHERNMOST POINTS

What you need:
- paper and pencil
- a compass

What to do between December 15 and 20:

1. Choose a time in the morning, such as when you're waiting for the school bus.
2. Choose a spot where you can sit and draw for a few minutes.
3. Check your compass and face east. (The sun should be slightly to your right.)
4. Sketch what you see around you— houses, trees, telephone poles—but not the sun.
5. Write *south* on the right side of the paper. Write *north* on the left side of your paper.
6. Make seven copies of your sketch on a copier machine. (See art above.)

What to do around the 21st of December, January, February, March, April, May, and June:

1. At the same time of day that you made your original sketch, go to your chosen spot with a pencil, compass, and one copy of your sketch.
2. Check your compass and face east.
3. Sketch the position of the sun. (Hint: In December, it should be slightly to your right. In March, it should be in front of you. In June, it should be slightly to your left.)
4. Write the date and time on each sketch.
5. After June 21st, put your sketches in order, from December to June.
6. Do your sketches show that:
   a. in December the sun was at its southernmost point in the sky?
   b. in March the sun was in the east?
   c. in June, the sun was at its northernmost point in the sky?

SHOW HOW THE TILT OF THE EARTH MAKES THE SEASONS

What you need:

- an orange (or ball of clay)
- a small lamp with the shade removed
- two toothpicks
- a black marker
- two thumbtacks

What to do:

1. Pretend the orange is the earth and the lamp is the sun.
2. Push one toothpick into the top of the orange. (That's the North Pole.)
3. Push the other toothpick into the bottom of the orange. (That's the South Pole.)
4. Draw a line around the middle of the orange. (That's the equator.)
5. Push a tack in halfway between the North Pole and the equator. (That's North America.)
6. Push a tack in halfway between the South Pole and the equator. (That's South America.)
7. Tilt the North Pole away from the sun. The North Pole is dark. It's winter in North America. The South Pole is sunny. It's summer in South America.
8. Keep the earth tilted the same way and move the orange one-quarter of the way around the sun. The sun shines equally on the North Pole and the South Pole. It's spring in North America and autumn in South America.
9. Keep the earth tilted the same way and move the orange another one-quarter of the way around the sun. The North Pole is sunny. It's summer in North America. The South Pole is dark. It's winter in South America.
10. Keep the earth tilted the same way and move the orange another one-quarter of the way around the sun. The sun shines equally on the North Pole and the South Pole. It's autumn in North America and spring in South America.

HAVE A WINTER SOLSTICE PARTY

1. Buy (or bake) 24 cupcakes, a bag of candy corn, and yellow icing.

2. Make your sun cupcakes glow.
   a. Frost each cupcake with yellow icing.
   b. Lay pieces of candy corn on top of the icing in a flower pattern to suggest the sun's rays.

3. Celebrate the solstice.
   a. Turn out the lights.
   b. Discuss how important sunlight is to life on earth.
   c. Put a lighted candle in each cupcake.
   d. Sing, *"We wish you a happy solstice.*
      We wish you a happy solstice.
      We wish you a happy solstice
      And a happy winter."
   e. Each person blows out a candle and makes a wish for the coming year.
   f. Enjoy the cupcake!

HAVE A WINTER SOLSTICE PARTY
FOR THE BIRDS

1. Put mini-doughnut-shaped cereal on a string, as though you are making a necklace. Roll the string of cereal in peanut butter. Shake the cereal string in a bag filled with birdseed.

2. Tie a string around a pinecone, leaving a loop at the top. Dip the pinecone in some peanut butter and roll it in birdseed.

3. Go outside to hang the bird feeders you've made. Sprinkle extra seeds on the ground, on stumps, and on rock ledges.

4. Discuss the ways that seeds represent life.

Further Reading

Jackson, Ellen B. *The Winter Solstice.*
Brookfield, CT: Millbrook Press, 1994.

Langstaff, Nancy, and John Langstaff, compilers.
The Christmas Revels Songbook, in Celebration of the Winter Solstice.
Boston, MA: David R. Godine, 1985.

Markle, Sandra. *Exploring Winter.*
New York, NY: Atheneum, 1984.

Morrison, Dorothy. *Yule: A Celebration of Light and Warmth.*
St. Paul, MN: Llewellyn Publications, 2000.

Web Sites

Additional information about solstice celebrations:
www.candlegrove.com/solstice.html

Fun quizzes and activities about the solstice:
www.familyeducation.com
(search for "winter solstice")